Let's Explore Pluto and Beyond

Helen and David Orme

Please visit our web site at: www.garethstevens.com
For a free color catalog describing our list of high-quality books, call 1-800-542-2595 (USA) or 1-800-387-3178 (Canada).
Our fax: (877) 542-2596

Library of Congress Cataloging-in-Publication Data

Orme, Helen.
Let's explore Pluto and beyond / Helen and David Orme.
p. cm. — (Space launch!)
Includes index.
ISBN-13: 978-0-8368-7945-2(lib. bdg.) ISBN-10: 0-8368-7945-7(lib. bdg.)
ISBN-13: 978-0-8368-8130-1 (softcover) ISBN-10: 0-8368-8130-3 (softcover)
1. Pluto (Planet)—Juvenile literature. I. Orme, David, 1948 Mar. 1- II. Title.
QB701.076 2007
523.48'2—dc22 2006035333

This North American edition first published in 2007 by
Gareth Stevens Publishing
A Weekly Reader® Company
1 Reader's Digest Road
Pleasantville, NY 10570-7000 USA

The publishers would like to thank: Sandra Voss, Tim Bones, James Powell, Indexing Specialists (UK) Ltd.

ticktock project editor: Julia Adams
ticktock project designer: Emma Randall

Gareth Stevens Editorial Direction: Mark Sachner
Gareth Stevens Editors: Carol Ryback and Barbara Kiely Miller
Gareth Stevens Art Direction: Tammy West
Gareth Stevens Designer: Dave Kowalski
Gareth Stevens Production: Jessica Yanke and Robert Kraus

Photo credits (t=top, b=bottom, c=center, l=left, r=right, bg=background)
Hubble Space Telescope: 20; Mary Evans: 19b; NASA: 1tl, 7t, 8 (all, 12 (original), 22, 23 (all); Science Photo Library: front cover, 1br, 4/5bg (original), 6 (original), 7b, 9t (original), 9b, 11tl, 13b, 14, 15 (all), 16, 17t, 18bl, 19tr; Shutterstock: 2/3bg, 11r, 24bg; Subaru Observatory: 21b; ticktock picture archive: 5tr, 6/7bg, 10/11bg, 10bl, 10br, 13t, 14/15bg, 17b, 18br, 18/19bg, 21t, 22/23bg. Rocket drawing Dave Kowalski/ © Gareth Stevens, Inc.

Printed in the United States of America

3 4 5 6 7 8 9 10 11 10 09 08

Contents

Words in the glossary are printed in **bold** the first time they appear in the text.

Where Is Pluto?

Pluto is part of the **solar system.** Like the eight known planets, Pluto travels around the Sun. Pluto is a **dwarf planet.**

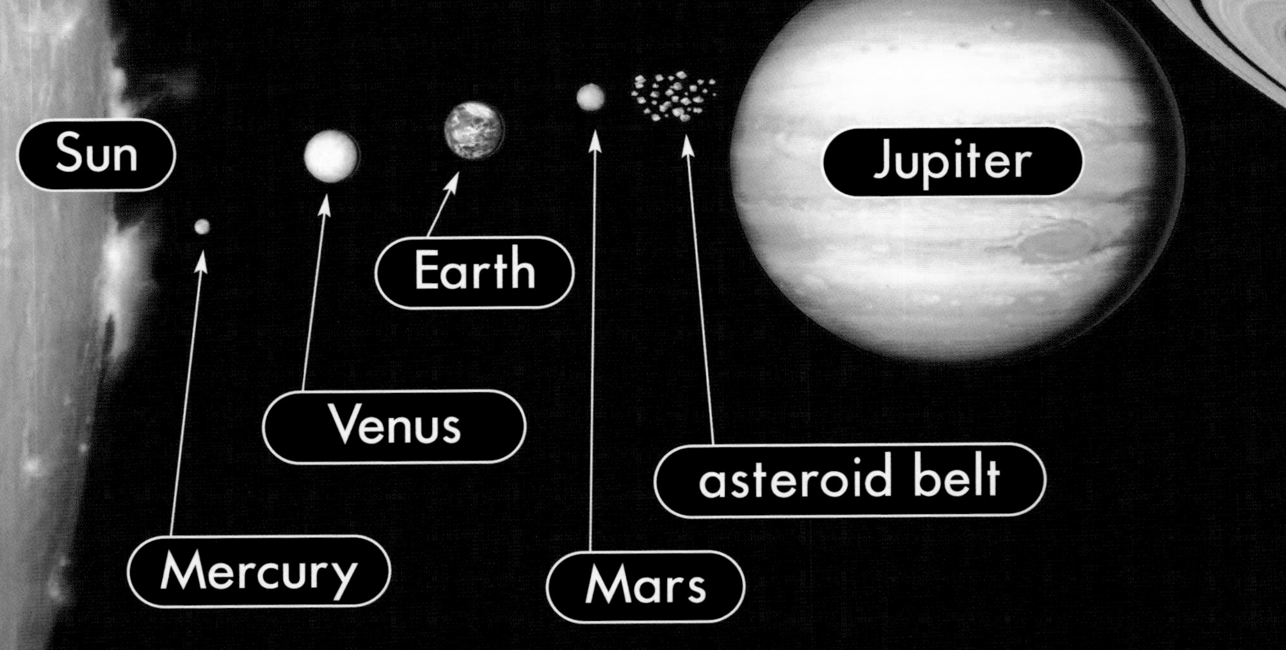

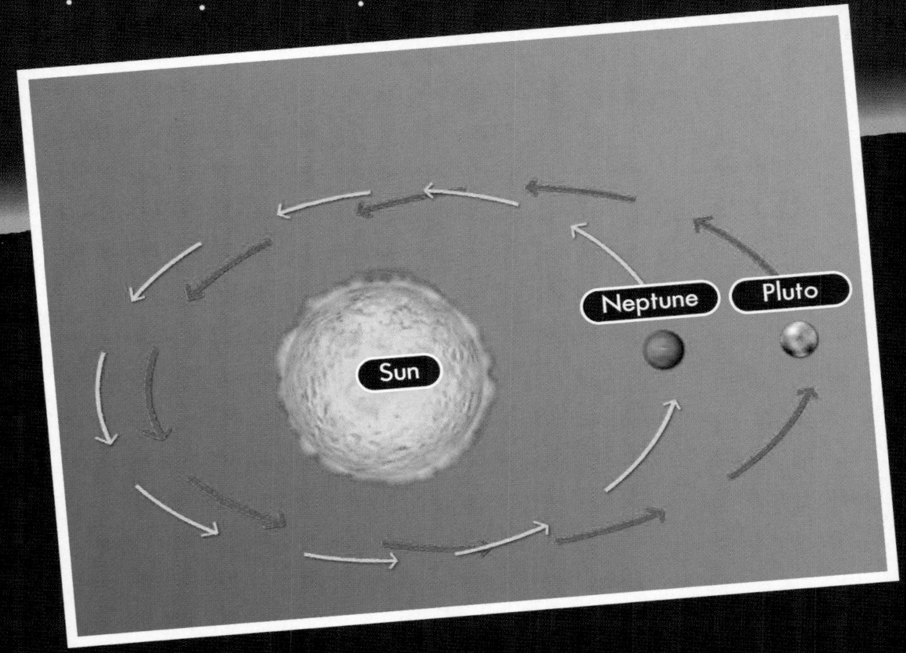

Pluto travels around the Sun once every 248 **Earth years**. This journey is called its **orbit**. The time it takes for a planet to travel around the Sun once is called a **year**. Sometimes, Pluto orbits closer to the Sun than Neptune.

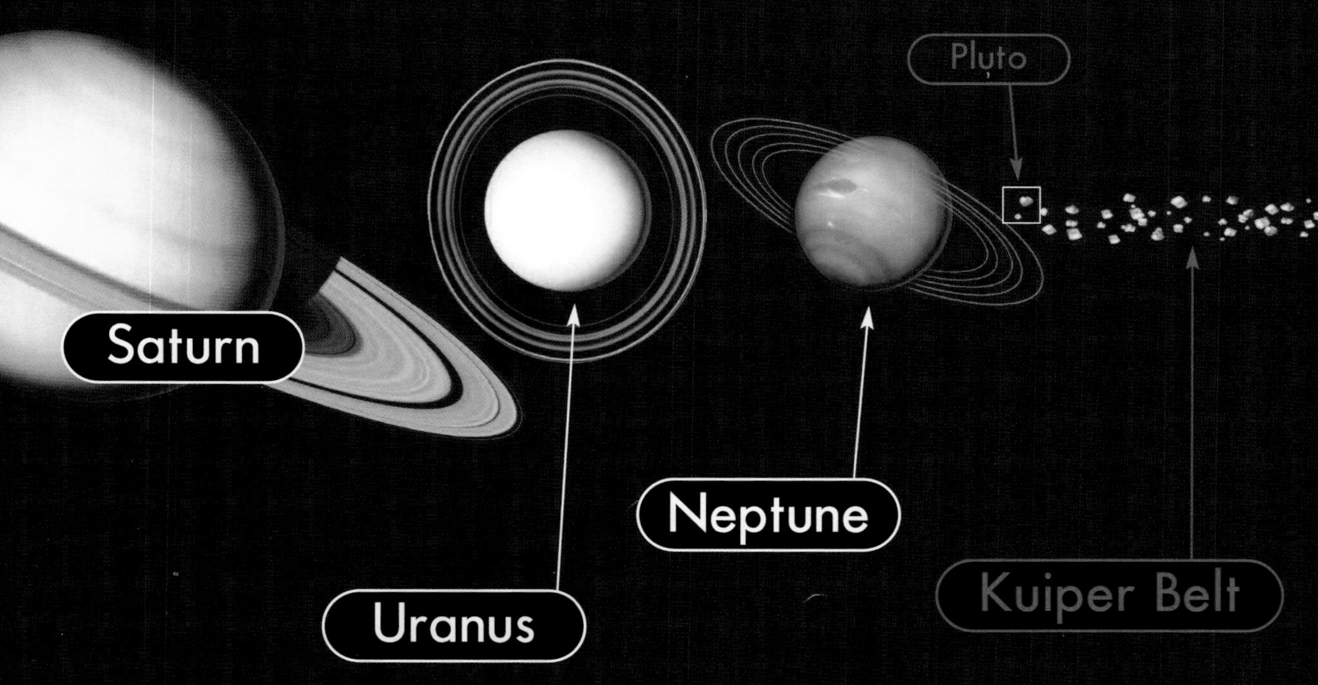

The Outer Solar System

Astronomers divide the solar system into inner and outer areas. Planets from Jupiter and beyond belong to the outer solar system.

Many other objects of different sizes are also part of the outer solar system. These objects are found in an area called the **Kuiper Belt**.

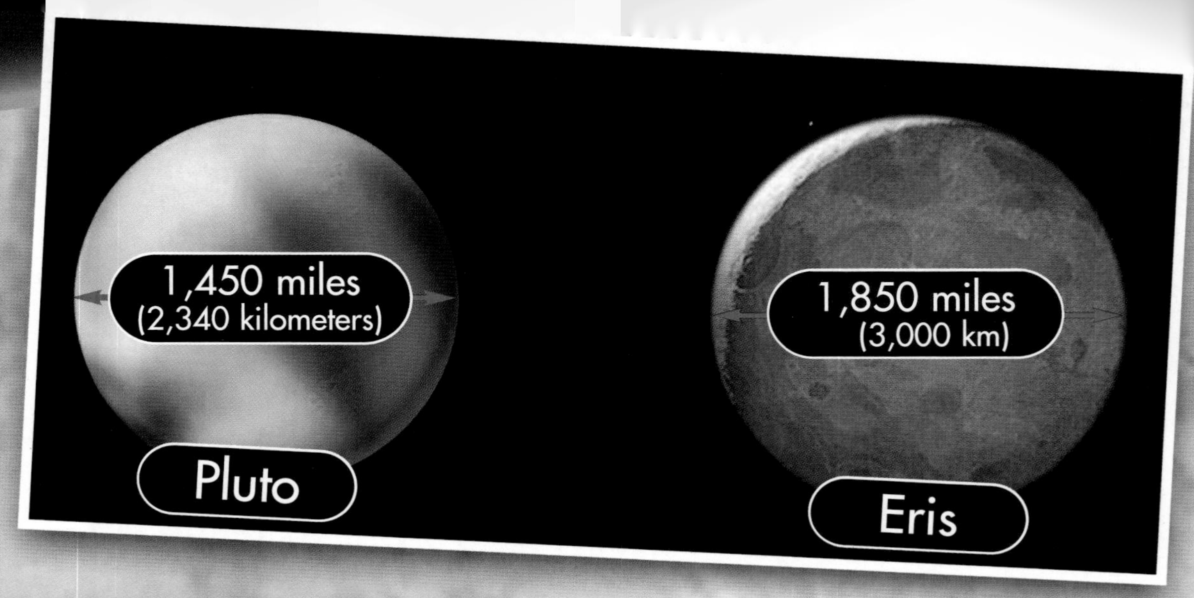

In 2005, astronomers discovered the dwarf planet called Eris. It is larger than Pluto.

Astronomers have no idea how many more dwarf planets they may discover in the Kuiper Belt.

Pluto: A Dwarf Planet

Pluto is smaller than some of the solar system's moons, including our own Moon.

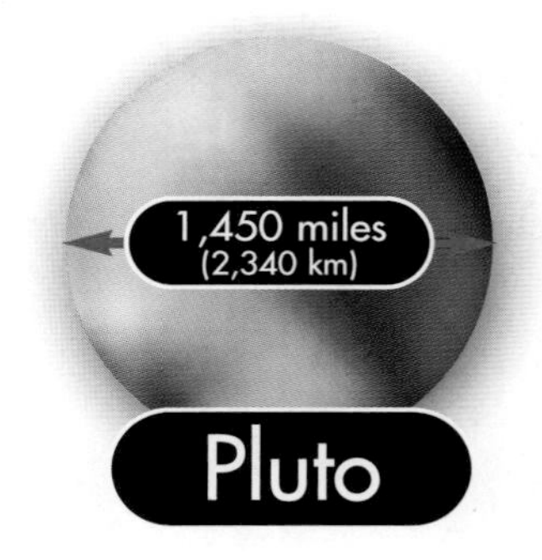

Pluto used to be called a planet. In 2006, astronomers took a vote about what to call Pluto. They decided that Pluto was really a dwarf planet.

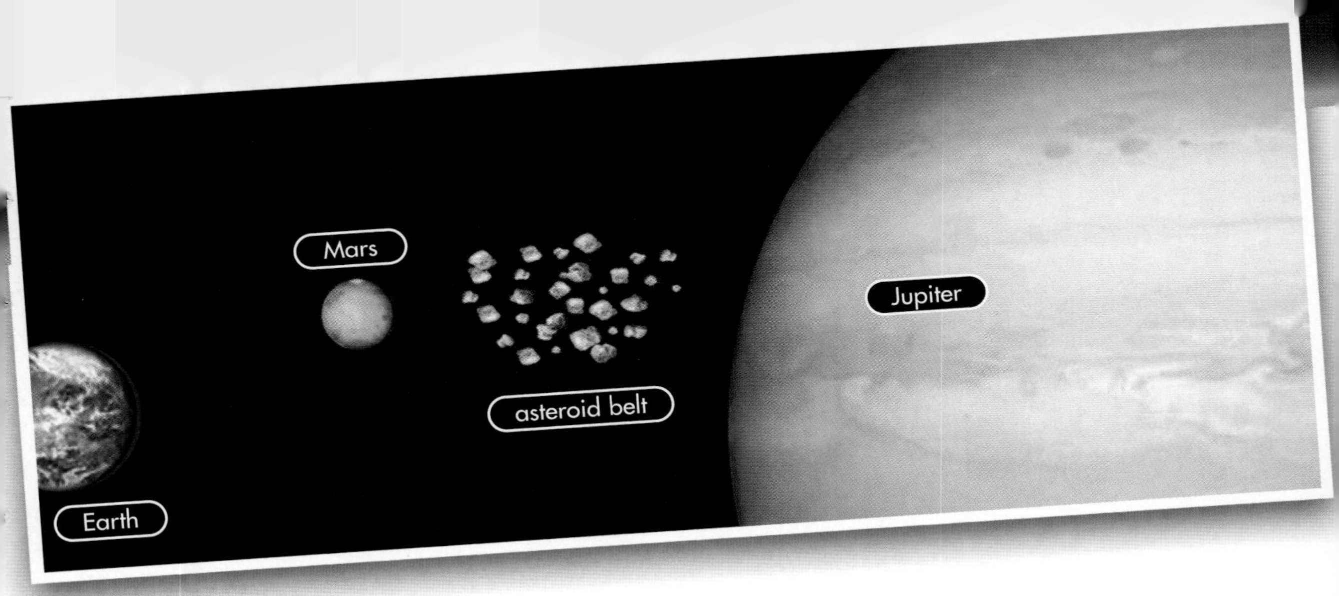

Most dwarf planets, like Pluto and Eris, are in the Kuiper Belt, which lies beyond Neptune. One dwarf planet is found in the **asteroid belt** between Mars and Jupiter.

Ceres, which is nearly 622 miles (1,001 km) across, is the dwarf planet found in the asteroid belt.

Dwarf Planet Facts

A dwarf planet is smaller than Mercury, our smallest planet. Astronomers must use special instruments to study dwarf planets, which are very far from Earth.

Even a powerful **telescope** shows Pluto as a tiny dot.

a view of Pluto from a Kuiper Belt object

Dwarf planets in the Kuiper Belt are probably made of rock and ice. Astronomers think that dwarf planets are covered with frozen gases called **methane** and **nitrogen**.

Dwarf planets are very cold places with extremely low temperatures. Kuiper Belt Objects are billions of miles (km) away from the heat and light of the Sun.

32° F

0° F

-100° F

-200° F

-300° F

-400° F

Water freezes at 32° Fahrenheit (0° Celsius)

The lowest temperature reached on Earth is -129° F (-89° C).

Temperatures on Pluto and Eris are probably about -380° F (-229° C).

What's the Weather Like?

The orbits of Pluto and Eris sometimes bring them closer to the Sun. More heat from the Sun changes a dwarf planet's weather.

Extra sunlight melts some of the frozen gases on Pluto and Eris. The **atmospheres** on dwarf planets get thicker when the temperatures rise.

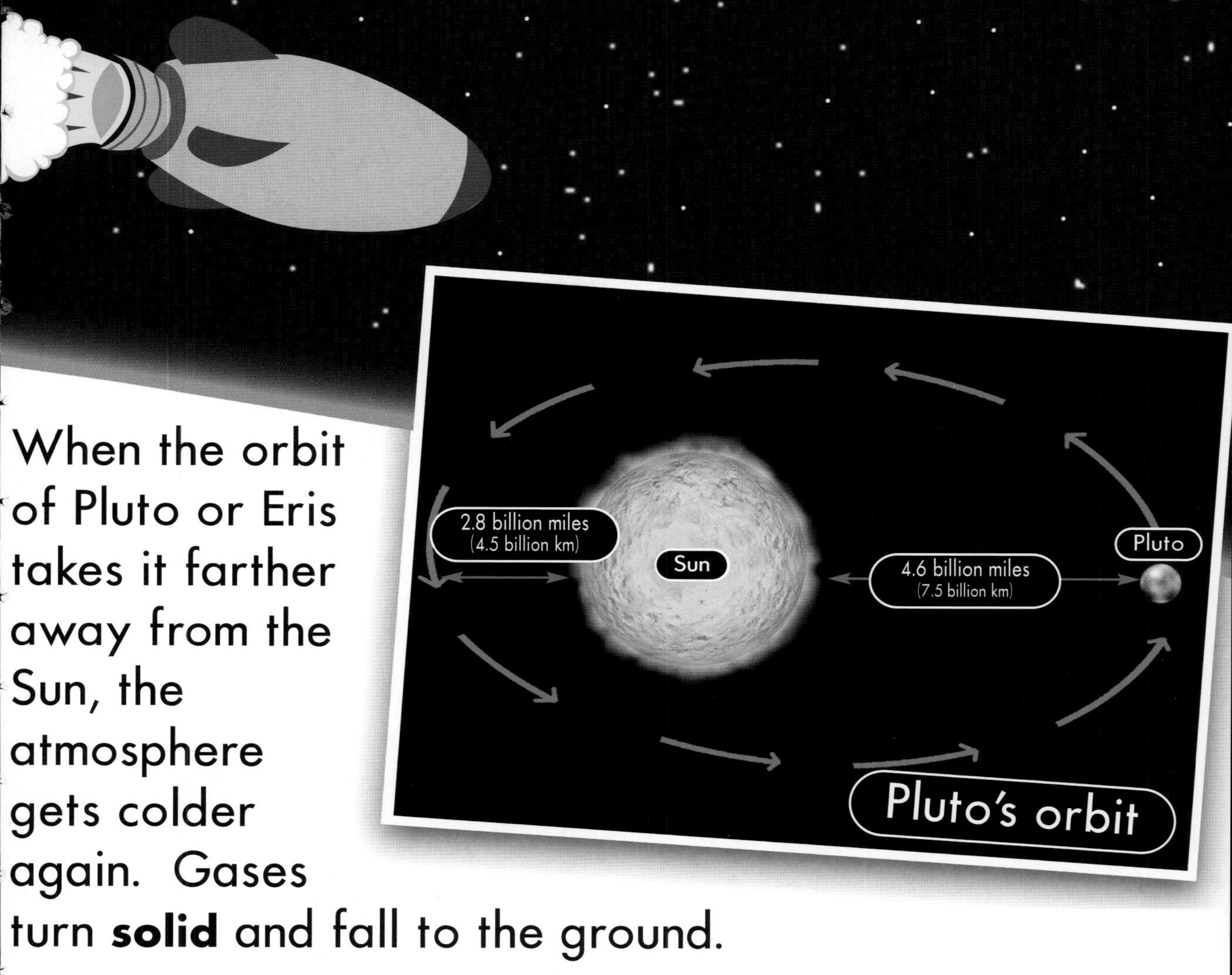

Pluto's orbit

When the orbit of Pluto or Eris takes it farther away from the Sun, the atmosphere gets colder again. Gases turn **solid** and fall to the ground.

Pluto's surface

As the freezing gases fall, the weather on Pluto and Eris might look just like snow on Earth!

Pluto's Moons

Pluto's main moon is Charon (pronounced "ka-ron"). It is about half as big as Pluto. Charon was discovered in 1978.

Some astronomers think Charon formed when a giant space object smashed into Pluto billions of years ago. Large pieces of Pluto may have broken off and become Charon.

Charon's surface is different from Pluto's. Charon's cold surface is made mostly of frozen water.

The Kuiper Belt

Far beyond the planets, more objects also orbit the Sun. Their place in space is called the Kuiper Belt.

Kuiper Belt Objects

The Kuiper Belt contains hundreds of thousands more objects than the asteroid belt. Kuiper Belt Objects are mostly small and made of ice.

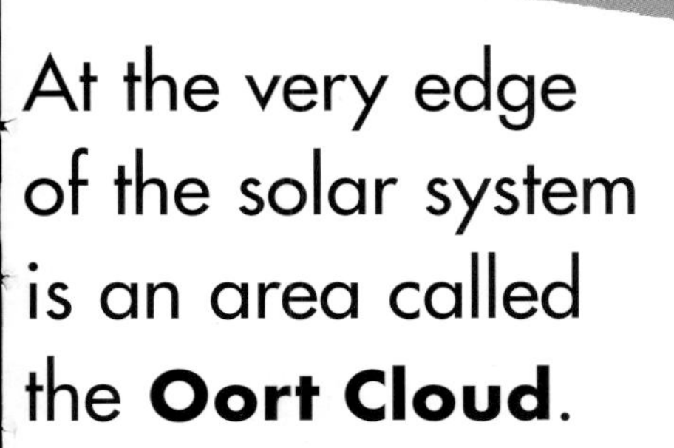

At the very edge of the solar system is an area called the **Oort Cloud**.

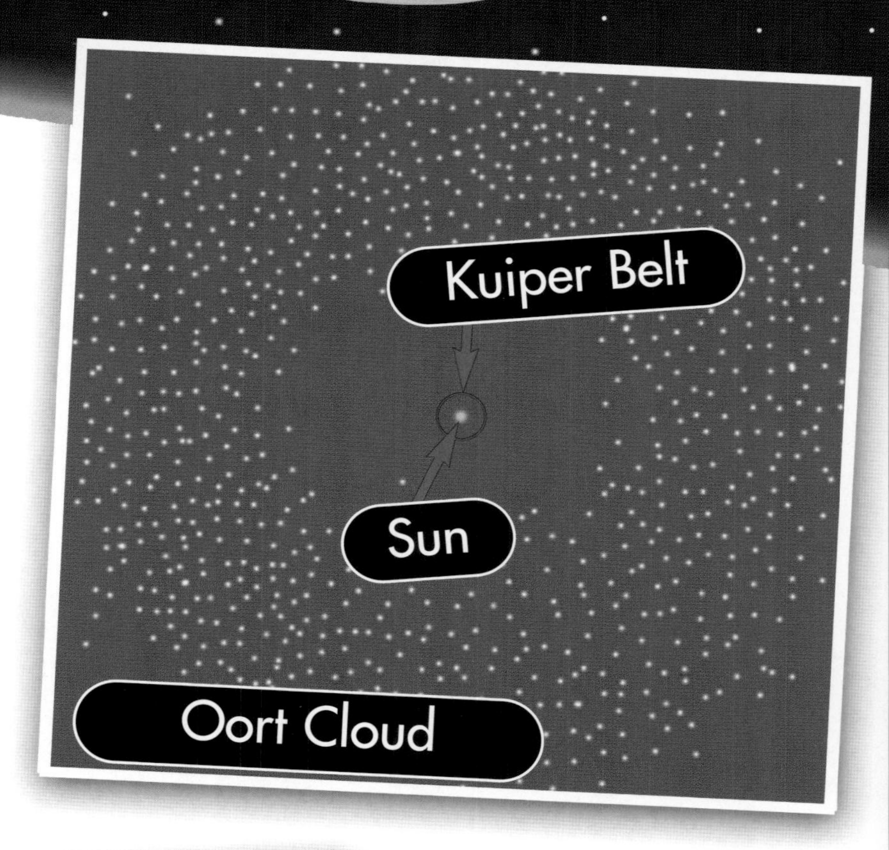

This drawing shows where the Oort Cloud is found.

Astronomers think **comets** start from the Oort Cloud area of the solar system.

Pluto in History

In the 1890s, astronomer Percival Lowell said there was another large object further out from the Sun than Neptune. He called it "Planet X."

Percival Lowell Observatory

Percival Lowell

Astronomers at the Percival Lowell **Observatory** in Flagstaff, Arizona, hunted for the new planet.

U.S. astronomer Clyde Tombaugh discovered Pluto in 1930.

Pluto was named after the Roman god of the **underworld**.

What Can We See?

Astronomers do not know much about Kuiper Belt Objects. They are too far away from Earth to study easily.

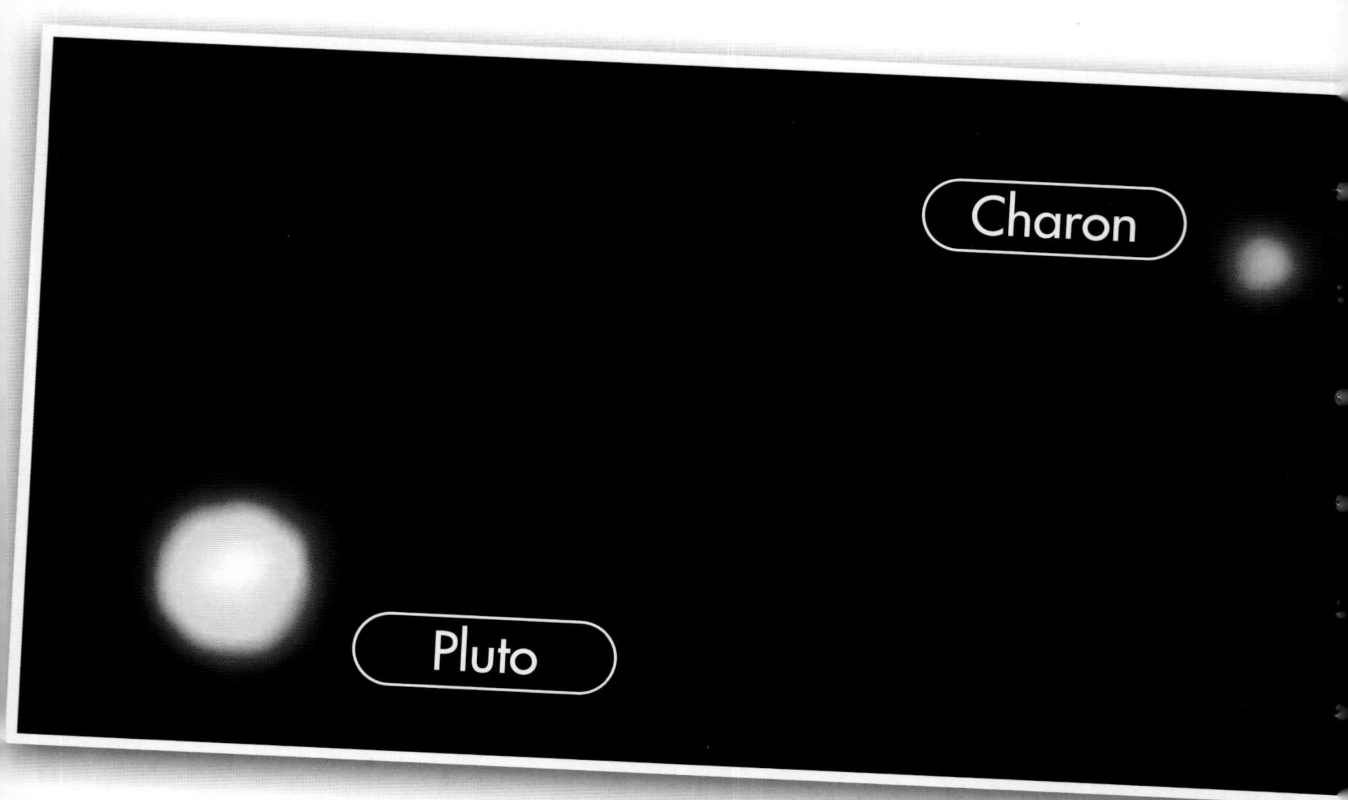

Here is one of the first pictures that shows Pluto and Charon together. The *Hubble Space Telescope,* which orbits Earth, took this picture in 1994.

Astronomers use the Subaru Observatory high on a mountaintop in Hawaii to study Pluto and other Kuiper Belt Objects.

Subaru Observatory

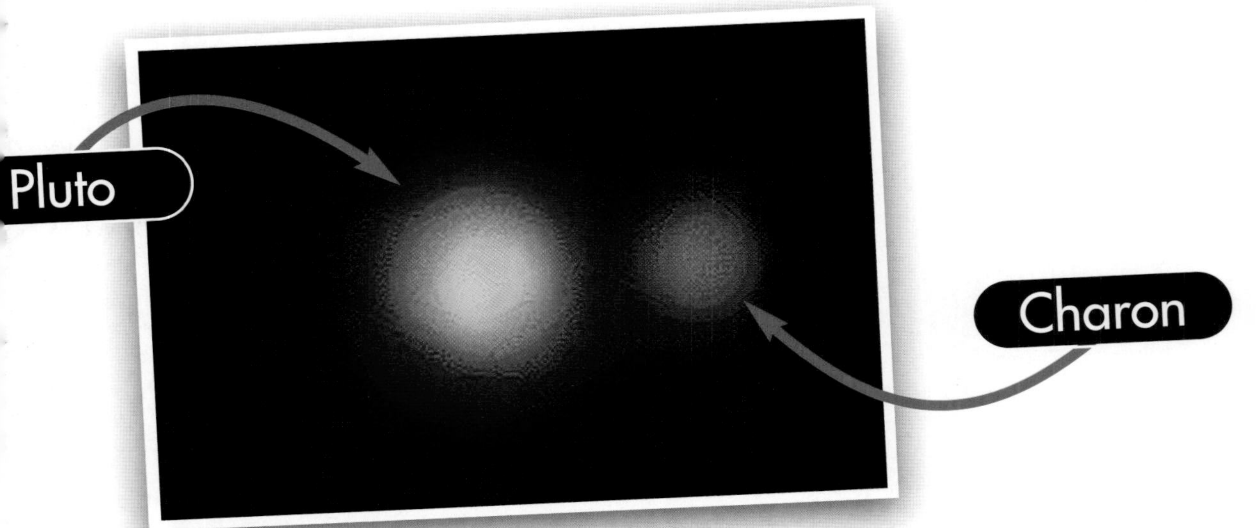

This photograph from the Subaru Observatory shows Pluto and Charon.

The New Horizons Mission

The *New Horizons* space probe was launched in January 2006. Its mission is to explore Pluto, Charon, and other Kuiper Belt Objects.

This picture shows the launch of the *New Horizons* mission from Cape Canaveral, Florida.

The *New Horizons* space probe should reach Pluto in 2015. It will study Kuiper Belt Objects during the years 2016 to 2020.

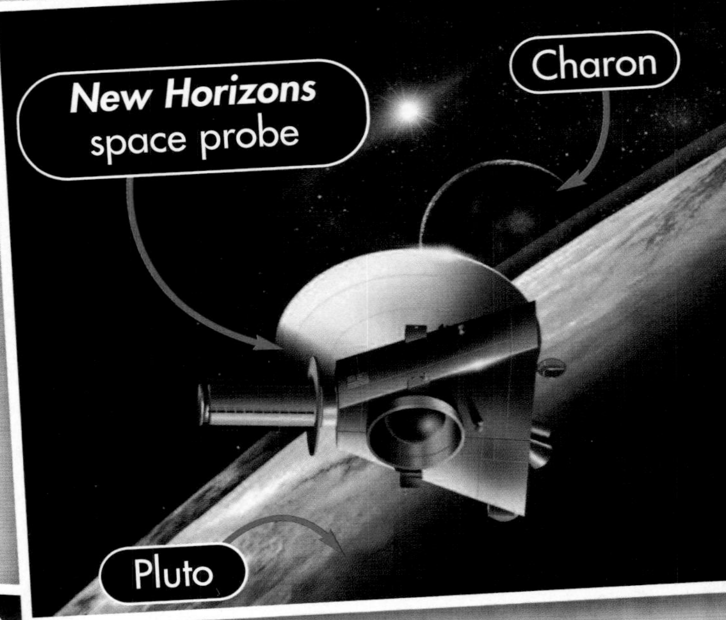

We still have a lot to learn about our solar system. Someday, you may be one of the astronomers who discovers new space objects!

Glossary

asteroid belt an area of space between Mars and Jupiter where a lot of rocky objects are found

astronomers scientists who study outer space, often using telescopes

atmosphere the gases that surround a planet, moon, or star

comets dusty ice balls that follow a wide orbit around the solar system

dwarf planet a planet smaller than Mercury

Earth year the time it takes Earth to orbit the Sun once (365 days)

Hubble Space Telescope a telescope that studies space from high above Earth's atmosphere

Kuiper Belt an area of space beyond Neptune

methane gas a gas with no smell that burns easily

nitrogen a gas found in many planets' atmospheres

observatory a building that houses huge telescopes and other astronomy equipment

Oort Cloud the area that marks the very edges of the solar system

orbit the path that one space object takes around another space object

solid a hard material

solar system the Sun and everything that is in orbit around it

space probe a spacecraft sent from Earth to explore the solar system

telescope an instrument used by astronomers to view space objects

underworld a mythical place for the dead

year the time it takes a planet to orbit the Sun

Index